i : Great Organ Case - west front

THE ORGAN OF GLOUCESTER CATHEDRAL

A Story in Pictures, Words and Sound by

John Balsdon

© 2010 John Balsdon
The Organ of Gloucester Cathedral

ISBN 978-0-9566089-0-1

Published by Willowhayne Books
11, Willowhayne Crescent
East Preston
West Sussex
BN16 1PJ

A CIP catalogue record of this book
can be obtained from the British Library.

Book designed by Michael Walsh at
THE BETTER BOOK COMPANY
5 Lime Close Chichester PO19 6SW
www.thebetterbookcompany.com

and printed by
ASHFORD COLOUR PRESS
Unit 600 Fareham Reach, Fareham Road, Gosport, Hants PO13 0FW

Contents

Preface

Gloucester Cathedral has been my spiritual home since the day I first walked into the building at the age of eight. I had been brought by my parents to attend voice trials in the hope of becoming a chorister here and as I stood in the warmth of the nave marvelling at the beauty of the huge Norman pillars, awestruck by the great height of the choir vault, I clearly remember saying to my father, "Dad, I'm coming here!" I am sure (although they never said) that this must have concerned my parents greatly as they had hoped that I would choose a cathedral choir nearer our home – Bristol or Wells for example, both of which had already offered me a place – so that I might not have to become a boarder and leave home. But no, Gloucester it had to be. So in 1959, I began my life-long acquaintance with and love of the building, its organ and its people. As a chorister under Dr Herbert Sumsion, I was fascinated by the wonderful sounds he would produce from the organ and being ever curious I would find myself investigating areas within the organ loft which were clearly out-of-bounds, to try to discover just how it worked. Thankfully, I was never caught!

It is with real joy therefore that I write this booklet. My first two chapters track the history of the instrument as an historical record. However in Chapter Three, I unashamedly change to the writing style of the first person, which marks the time from which I first came to Gloucester; I simply could not avoid including personal memories of my own and of the many who have played the instrument up to the present day. Chapter Six returns to an historical appraisal of the wonderful organ cases and is based on original material by Herbert and John Norman from the 1971 booklet.

Finally, I have gone one step further by including a CD of the organ as it sounded back in 1950, through to today's fine additions – a souvenir of moments and sounds in time which I sincerely hope the reader and listener will enjoy.

John Balsdon
East Preston, West Sussex,
July 2010

Foreword

My first memories of the Gloucester Cathedral Organ date from the Three Choirs Festival of 1971, when I was singing as a *Worcester* Cathedral Chorister.

I had grown up loving the sound of Worcester's magnificent old organ relic, with its Tubas and Bombardes, and it was apparent even to a twelve year old boy during the 1971 Festival, that the then new Gloucester organ was very different. My memory is that I heard nothing but complaints about it that week. 'Why no 32 footer for the end of that Nunc Dimittis?' 'Why no solo reed?' 'Why no solo clarinet for such and such?' These were the questions which I heard asked during that festival over and over again.

John Sanders and Ralph Downes had, however, created something very new for an English Cathedral. In the words of Seiriol Evans's articulate and reasonable foreword to the 1971 Organ Booklet, they had re-designed the organ 'to bring it into line with musical thought about the function and capacity of organs in the present day.' It was, Dean Evans added, 'an organ of the *seventies*, and as such it should be appraised.'

Well, much of what was created in the 1970s is these days greeted with scorn. Forty years on, however, many organ lovers agree that the Gloucester organ is a unique and beautiful instrument, and not at all a victim of the cultural vandalism of that decade. It may not have many of the sounds which are appropriate for the Anglican Cathedral choral repertoire, but an enormous range of solo organ music can be performed on it with thrilling effect; and skilled accompanists can create many of the effects associated with more traditional English Cathedral organs.

Tastes in organ design evolve however, and priorities change. I believe that nobody in 2010 would design an English cathedral organ like this one, in which from a distance of forty years, it seems that contemporary organ building dogma took precedence over musical practicalities.

Without in any way compromising the integrity of the instrument, David Briggs made some much-needed changes in 1998. I believe that the addition of a Solo Reed this year, will similarly *add* to the instrument's glory. There may be more additions in the next few years – funds permitting – again, only to add some more Anglican colour to the organ, without destroying the principles upon which it was designed in the 1970s. After all, the organ has to fulfil may functions here – different functions from those of an organ in 18ᵗʰ century Germany, for example.

I am grateful to John Balsdon for writing this new account of the history of the organ in Gloucester Cathedral. It is written in a subjective and engaging way and evinces John's great knowledge of, and love for, the music making in Gloucester Cathedral. His love I share, for it is a privilege to work in this exceptionally beautiful building, whose acoustics have the power to make even ordinary sounds seem beautiful; and one thing is certain, the Gloucester Cathedral Organ could never be described as *ordinary*!

Adrian Partington, Director of Music
Gloucester Cathedral, May 2010

CHAPTER ONE
DALLAM AND HARRIS:
THE ENGLISH "CLASSICAL" ORGAN: 1640 – 1847

Standing proudly on the screen in this most magnificent of cathedrals, the beautiful 17th century organ cases continue to amaze visitors and worshippers 350 years after their completion. Those fortunate enough to hear this unique instrument are treated to combinations of warm, rich flutes and diapasons, fiery reeds and brilliant mixtures which, all combined, produce a thrilling full organ sound or "tutti" enhanced by the building's unique eight-second reverberation. But listeners are often unaware that even today, over 200 pipes from the organ built in 1666 live on and speak to us just as they did when they were first placed in these beautiful cases.

How can this be? Miraculously, the two organ cases at Gloucester escaped the destruction which religious upheaval, changes in architectural fashion and violence from reckless troops forced on so many of their contemporaries. The colours of the 17th century painted decoration on the pipes, pipe-shades and cornices, restored in 1970, take us back in time to another age. We will journey back to that time now to trace the origins of the Gloucester organ.

The main or "great" case (see picture i) of the organ was built by Thomas Harris and dates from 1666. The east and west fronts still contain their original painted pipes. Today, these very pipes produce the fundamental tones of the Great organ just as they did in the 17th century. Chapter 6 provides a detailed consideration of the Gloucester cases and their restoration.

The smaller "chair" case on the east side over the entrance to the quire is of a style markedly different from that of its companion up above. Experts for many years have ascribed it to the organ builder Thomas Dallam, dating its construction to the latter half of the 16th century – considerably older than Harris' work.

If this dating is accurate, then this chair case is indeed a rare survival. It is believed that only a handful of churches in Britain possess organ cases dating from before the Commonwealth, when so many instruments were destroyed, dismantled or left to decay following the English Civil War.

ii : Chair Case

iii : the Quire, showing the organ in its original position

Cathedral records are not complete prior to 1663, but we can speculate that when it was built, Dallam's new organ at Gloucester was placed in a loft above the choir stalls, under the double arches between the quire and the south transept. There still exists in the stonework, evidence of supports for the loft. There was also a tracing by F. S. Waller of a painting (sadly now lost) showing the quire with its early 18th century woodwork with the organ in this original position.

A visitor to Gloucester, one Celia Fiennes, came to the cathedral during her journey in 1698 *(The Journeys of Celia Fiennes,* edited by Christopher Morris, 1947, p. 234). She says *"The Cathedral or Minster is large lofty and very neate, the Quire pretty; at the entrance there is a seate over head for the Bishop to sit in to hear the sermon preached in the body of the Church, and therefore the Organs in the Quire was on one side which used to be at the entrance"*.

This seems to indicate that the pre-1663 *"organs"* had been on the screen like the early organs in Windsor Chapel. But it is not clear whether our visitor meant that those same organs were now on the side, or just that the organ in its new form was placed in this new position.

We have no precise account of any of the organs before 1663, but we do have various records of payments prior to Thomas Harris coming on the scene. For instance – in 1635, *"To Tho. Bull for mendinge the organs 01. 10. 00"*; and to players, such as that in 1638 *"To John Roberts My Lord Bishopps servant for playing on the organs att severall tymes 00. 10. 00"*. So the cathedral then contained at least one instrument.

The early 17th century organs at Gloucester were evidently not much cherished. When William Laud was installed Dean in 1616 he found them "in great decay and in a short time likely to be of noe use". The Chapter Act Book records a letter signed by him with two other members of the Chapter on March 12th, 1616 and circulated among the great and the good of the county. It describes the organs as *"very meane, and besides that very farr decayed, which is a great blemishe to the solemnity of the service of God in that place. We are at this time repayringe the decayes of the church and are utterly disinabled to provide a new organe without the helpe of such worthy gentlemen and others well disposed as shall approve our indeavour. We are ledd on upon this adventure by the example of our neighbour church of Worcester, which (though it be farr better able than ours is) yett found this burden too heavye for them and therefore took this course with good success to the greate honour of the Gentrye and other Inhabitants of that Sheire".*

The accounts for 1639-1640 show that at last something was done. Thomas Cooke was paid 2s. *"for assuring the organ loft and goeing three or four miles for newe timber for it"*; and 6s. was given to *"a messenger to Worcester twoe or severall tymes to Mr. Thomkins about the agreemt with Dallam for the new organ."* This *Mr Thomkins*, a Gloucester boy, would have been the son of Thomas Tomkins, the composer.

Cooke was also paid 10s.9d. for taking down the old organ, and 6s.8d. was paid to *"Coward Meason, Sadler, for leather and mending the organ bellowes"*. Of the new Dallam organ itself no description survives, but it was "approved" by Tomkins in 1641.

The years of the Great Rebellion are marked by a gap in the accounts which begin again in 1660 with an army of workmen – carpenters, joiners, glaziers, plumbers, masons – at work on refurbishing the building and its fittings. It is not recorded that Dallam's organ had been destroyed and when we read an entry (1661-2) of £80 paid *"to Mr. Yate for the Organ"* it looks as though it had been sold and was now being re-purchased. £10 was paid *"to Taynton for tuninge and settinge up the organ"*. Taynton (or Taunton) was a Bristol organ-builder to whom the newly-appointed Gloucester organist, Robert Webb, had just paid a visit at a cost to the Cathedral of £1 2s 6d. As it had cost £80 two years before it is possible that the case was kept for re-use and only the pipes and works sold. It may well be that the reason for the re-purchasing of this older case, used for a part of the new organ, is that it would have saved the Cathedral precious funds.

The price of £80 would indicate a small organ, possibly of one manual only. Its specification would have been typical of pre-Restoration instruments, with no reeds or mixtures. There are payments in the 17th century accounts to players of the *"sagbutts and cornetts"*, but these ceased to be necessary when the revival of organ-building in the 1660s introduced the use of reeds and mixtures.

For two years the Dean and Chapter used the organ they had bought back from Mr. Yate, but as part of the restoration of the Cathedral services, a new organ was evidently needed. So, on October 26th, 1663 we have the record of £40 *"to Mr. Tho. Harris towards the new organ he is to make, this being pd at ye ensealinge of the Articles"*. It is these very articles which enabled work to commence, by Thomas Harris, on the Great case which we see today on the screen.

Although the Articles themselves have not been preserved, the account books happily enable the progress of the work to be followed, and show that the craftsmen already employed in the Cathedral did much of the structural work and probably the carving. The most important of the *"joyners"* was one Thomas Ellridge, who in 1662 worked on *"the fframe of the great Bell Wheele"*. He appears throughout the entries concerning the new Harris instrument.

Thomas Harris had returned to England at this time after a period in France and the Low Countries. He brought back experience of the traditions from the Continent and worked in many of our English Cathedrals. Robert Dallam, too, spent the Commonwealth years abroad in Brittany and his sister married Thomas Harris, establishing the Dallam/Harris family connection.

The entries for the payments to Harris show that he received a total of about £400 for his work. Money was raised by appeals to friends and tenants of the Dean and Chapter, so it was decided to commemorate their generosity by decorating the display pipes with their various Coats-of-Arms.

iv : East Great pipes detail

A local painter, John Campion, was employed for the work, and there is an entry in the 1663-4 accounts of £5 *"pd Mr. Campion toward the 85 li agreed on to be pd him for the gylding painting the new organ"*.

The final account for the new organ shows £82 from subscribers, among whom are the Marquess of Dorchester and the Earl of Southampton, and there is a further entry *"Reed of the Ld Bp of Oxon as his guift towards the ffurniture stopp upon the Organ 10 li wch was pd Mr. Harris"*. Harris was paid £100, and £10 as the gratuity. Mr Campion had £13 and a further £17 in the next year's account (1666-1667). His work was not fully paid for until 1669, when on

15th December he had £2 *"towards money remayneing for the organ"*. The bellows of the organ were not yet cased, and rats were a nuisance: in November, Mr Jordan was paid 2s.6d. *"for medicines for the ratts that troubled the Organ Bellars"*. In 1666 this was put right, and £3 paid out *"for the Organ Bellowes Case not charged before"*.

After Thomas Harris had finished his work the history of the organ becomes more difficult to follow as things did not go entirely to plan in terms of reliability! It is quite astonishing to read that only in 1667 there is a payment to *"Mr. Maynard for mending the stopps of the Chayre organ"*. Harris was also paid £4 for mending the organ.

Then in 1674, we have the first mention of preventative maintenance. The Dean and Chapter made an agreement with Thomas Harris and *"Rene (Renatus) Harris his sonne"* that for a yearly sum of £5 they would *"well and sufficiently keepe the organ in as good repaire as it now is especially as to the musique part of it also to keepe it from Runninges Stickinges and Cipheringes or whatever else may happen to the prejudice of the said organ all violent mocons or accidents by ropes and prejudice by Ratts and other Vermin excepted"*. Several other Cathedral accounts of this period show unusually large sums being spent on repairs to or servicing of the new organ. We should remember that in 1666 Harris was building three major organs, Gloucester, Salisbury and Worcester. This father and son team might just have taken on too much in those early days.

The care and maintenance of the Gloucester instrument between 1687 and Willis' arrival on the scene in 1847 moved from organ builder to organ builder. In 1687 Harris' great rival Bernard Smith was paid £150 in two instalments. There is an entry in the Chapter Acts ordering *"seaventy pounds remaynng due to Mr. Barnard Smith for Repaire of the Organs to be paid by the Treasurer out of the first moneys that come to his hands"*. Smith continued to look after the organs until within a year or two of his death, and from 1705 to 1707 Christian Smith succeeded him. Abraham Jordan did work in 1708, but fell out with the Dean and Chapter who then ordered that *"if there be any further business or work to be done to the organ Mr. Thomas Swarbrick shall have the refusal of it".*

According to the Rev. T. D. Fosbrooke, the Gloucester historian writing in 1819, the organ was moved to its present position over the west door of the quire in 1718. At that date Abbot Wigmore's pulpitum was pulled down and the *"square stone pulpit"* which Celia Fiennes mentioned was destroyed, its place being taken by the organ. The Gloucester Corporation Minutes of 1717 approved a present of £50 to the Dean, as a contribution to his *"work of large expence by Beautifying and Enlarging the Choir"* for the better accommodation of the Corporation and Citizens—and specifically for moving the organ. As Thomas Swarbrick seems to have cared for the organ until 1720 it is most likely that he undertook the work of removal.

Swarbrick had worked for Renatus Harris and on his own account built the fine organs at Birmingham, St. Philip, (now the Cathedral) and Warwick, St. Mary. His organ-cases were much influenced in design by those of Harris. He was followed at Gloucester by Richard Bridge, John Snetzler (who was paid £130 for repairs in 1757), the younger Byfield and John Avery.

In 1787 Robert and William Gray visited Gloucester to examine the organ and to estimate for repairs. Their work would have been considerable as they were paid £6 6s. 0d. for the journey to make the estimate and £241 in 1790 for the work itself. At the same time Richard Barrett was paid £34 15s. 2d. for *"new painting gilding and beautifying the organ previous to the Music Meeting this Year"*.

The specification of the organ as left by the Grays was recorded in the early 19th century by J. H. Leffler and printed in C. W. Pearce's *Notes on English Organs*. This is the earliest specification we have of the Gloucester organ, and I am indebted to John Norman, who has kindly provided a picture of this extract from the original manuscript:-

Glocester Cathedral.

Organ suppos'd to have been built by Schmidt – since repair'd by Gray. – has three setts of Keys. from G. to GG. long Octaves. – Swell to F. –

Great

Open Diaps — 58
Open Diaps — 58
Stop Diaps — 58
Principal — 58
Twelfth — 58
Fifteenth — 58
Sesq.ª 4 ranks 232
Trumpet — 58
Corn.ᵗ to C 5 ranks 150
—————
788

Choir

Stop Diaps — 58
Principal — 58
Flute — 58
Fifteenth — 58
Voxhum.ᵉ — 58
—————
290

Swell

Open Diaps — 37
Stop Diaps — 37
Principal — 37
Cornet 3 ranks 131
Trumpet — 37
Hautboy — 37
—————
296
290
788
—————
1374

Organist M.ʳ Mutlow

10 Bells Tenor 60 Cwt.

Leffler manuscript specification, 1792

After 1808, when the Grays ceased to look after the organ, Corfield, Traherne, Flight & Robson and Flight & Barr successively did works of maintenance. Then around 1830 J. C. Bishop made improvements and additions. According to a contemporary *Treatise on the Organ* by Joshua Done these included the enlargement of the Swell and the provision of pedal pipes. These pipes form the pedal rank "Flute 16" on today's instrument and for many years were understood to have been the largest-scale 16 foot open wood pipes in the country.

v : Bishop Pedal pipes (wood)

We have now arrived at the year 1847 when the young Henry Willis arrives at Gloucester.

9

CHAPTER TWO

FATHER WILLIS:

THE CLASSICAL ORGAN AND THE "MODERN" INSTRUMENT: 1847 – 1919

The next significant rebuilding of the instrument was undertaken in 1847 by Henry Willis. He had just restored the organ at Tewkesbury Abbey and in later life recalled his work at Gloucester as his "stepping-stone to fame". This work marks the start of the "modern" history of the Gloucester organ. The Great was extended down to CCC and a new Swell was added comprising twelve stops down to CC. The Swell organ boasted a double venetian front which produced a pianissimo that Willis described as "simply outstanding". He goes on to say "I received £400 for the job and was presumptuous enough to marry".

The 1847 Willis specification was:

vi : Father Willis

GREAT ORGAN	SWELL ORGAN	CHOIR ORGAN
CCC *to* F, 66 *notes*	CC *to* F, 54 *notes*	GG *(no GG Sharp)* *to* F, 58 *notes*
Open Diapason	Open Diapason	
Open Diapason	Open Diapason	Dulciana
Stopped Diapason	Stopped Diapason	Stopped Diapason
Clarabella	Dulciana	Principal
Principal	Principal	Flute (metal)
Twelfth	Flute	Fifteenth

Fifteenth	Fifteenth	
Sesquialtera IV	Sesquialtera	
Mixture II (new)	Trumpet	
Trumpet (new)	Hautboy	PEDAL ORGAN
Clarion	Cremona	*CCC to E 29 notes*
	Clarion	Pedal Pipes

Usual couplers, but no Swell to Pedal. "Pedals to Great" was given twice.

vii : Willis voicing a pipe

The design of this "father" Willis organ was still firmly rooted in the English classical tradition. Willis had been apprenticed to Gray & Davison, successors to Robert and William Gray, and during the course of a long career was to rebuild all the cathedral organs in South-West England save that of Bristol. His Gloucester instrument must have sounded much improved from its predecessors and would have delighted all those who heard it. We should remember that at this time the soundboards were still oriented on a north-south axis so that the instrument spoke mainly into the quire – just as Harris' original instrument had done. Its specification is not just rich in

11

foundation stops, but appears wonderfully comprehensive and flexible for the player. The huge scale Bishop pedal pipes would have provided a solid foundation upon which to build the manual chorus. The player too was situated perfectly for quire services – between the great and chair cases, facing west into the organ case. The action would have been tracker throughout. The picture below from 1850 shows Willis' instrument with the addition of gothic pinnacles placed on the towers of the case – a design trend which happily fell out of fashion by the 20th century!

viii : the Organ circa 1850

This was the instrument upon which Dr S. S. Wesley and Dr C. H. Lloyd played during the whole of their successive tenures of the post of Cathedral Organist. Willis kept the organ in good shape for Wesley until the latter's death in 1876. When Lloyd took up his post in 1876, services in the nave were being introduced. Playing for nave services on the east side of the case would have been challenging in the extreme. Lloyd therefore obtained permission to ask Willis to conduct a thorough inspection and to suggest ways in which the instrument could cope better with both quire and nave services. Willis cited the Exeter and King's College Cambridge solutions to the nave problem – the organist sitting to one side – having direct visual contact with both nave and quire. This was to be another major project. The Dean and Chapter agreed to donate £500 towards the work of rebuilding the instrument, but in 1878 the whole idea was postponed and a major clean was undertaken instead.

Charles Lee Williams became organist in 1882 and immediately began to press for action to be taken to overcome the difficulties of nave accompaniment and by 1886 the decision was taken. This was not an easy time to raise money as the country was suffering an agricultural depression and there was little money that the Chapter could give. Despite this, the Chapter decided to launch an appeal for the rebuilding of a new instrument in 1888. The screen was not to be altered nor the organ cases nor the "old mellow stops or in any way the position of the organ".

Henry Willis commenced work on a complete rebuild in 1888 and on the 10th January 1889 there was a dedication service to give thanks for the rebuilt and enlarged instrument.

To make the organ comfortably useful for services and other musical events in the nave, Willis provided a new console on the south side. Then, in an attempt to ensure that the instrument could be heard equally well both in the quire and nave, he turned his new soundboards within the main case through ninety degrees so that they ran from east to west. The soundboards and mechanism of the old organ had become w o r m – e a t e n a n d dilapidated, but there was neither the room nor the funding for a really large cathedral instrument. So, in his Great and Swell, a higher wind pressure was used to obtain *"the effect of a much larger organ"* whilst the chair organ was *"left to its fate"* as a relatively unimportant architectural curiosity. The pedal pipes added by Bishop were placed within the arch to the aisle on the north side. The new action to Great, Swell and Pedal was pneumatic but that

ix : typical Father Willis stop jamb
– not Gloucester

to the Choir organ (still in the chair case facing east) was tracker. Not only was the organist now in the best position to view both the nave and quire, but all the pipes within the case spoke directly to him. Picture ix shows a Willis stop jamb of the same vintage as his rebuilt organ at Gloucester.

The specification, which included several stops *"prepared for"* until funds became available, was as follows:-

GREAT ORGAN, CC to A

Double diapason, metal	16
Open diapason, metal	8
Open diapason, metal	8
Claribel flute, wood	8
Principal, metal	4
Flute harmonique, metal	4
Twelfth, metal	2 ²/₃
Fifteenth, metal	2
Sesquialtera, metal	III
★Trombone, metal	16
Trumpet, metal	8
Clarion, metal	4

CHOIR ORGAN, CC to A

Dulciana	8
Stopped diapason	8
Principal	4
Flute	4
Clarinet	8

PEDAL ORGAN, CCC to F

Open diapason, wood	16
Bourdon, wood	16
★Octave, wood	8
★Ophicleide, metal	16

SWELL ORGAN, CC to A

Double diapason, wood and metal	16
Open diapason, metal	8
Salicional, metal	8
Vox angelica (tenor C), metal	8
Lieblich gedact, wood and metal	8
Gemshorn, metal	4
Fifteenth, metal	2
Mixture, metal	III
★Contra posaune, metal	16
Cornopean, metal	8
Hautboy, metal	8
Clarion, metal	4

★Prepared for only

COUPLERS

Swell to Great   Great to Pedals
Choir to Great   Choir to Pedals
Swell to Pedals

ACCESSORIES

4 composition Pedals to Great
3 composition Pedals to Swell
1 double-acting pedal for Great to
Pedals
Radiating and concave pedal-board

In 1896, Lee Williams resigned his post due to failing health. He was not to see through the completion of Willis' scheme for the instrument, as that would be for his successor Dr Herbert Brewer, who was appointed immediately, much to the great delight of many local Gloucester people. Brewer had been the most distinguished of Lloyd's pupils, a brilliant organist and importantly a Gloucester boy. Within six months of Brewer's taking up his post, he began an initiative to complete the organ to Willis' final specification. Thus the year of 1898 saw the final enlargement of the instrument by Willis. A new Solo organ was added, in a swell box situated behind the console at the southern end of the screen and those stops which had been prepared for in 1888 were installed. The Ophicleide and Octave were also positioned next to the Solo box. In addition, a new pedal board was installed and the Choir organ soundboard was replaced.

After these latter improvements the specification was:—

GREAT ORGAN		SWELL ORGAN		SOLO ORGAN	
As before, but complete		As before, but complete		Flute	8
				Clarinet	8
CHOIR ORGAN		COUPLERS		Orchestral Oboe	8
Stopped diapason	8	Solo to Great		Tuba Mirabilis	8
Dulciana	8	Swell to Great			
Flute	4	Choir to Great		PEDAL ORGAN	
Clarinet	8	Solo to Pedal		As before, but complete	
Cor anglais	8	Swell to Pedal			
(in place of the Principal)		Great to Pedal		ACCESSORIES	
		Choir to Pedal		As before	

It is a pity that recording facilities were not yet invented to record the sound of this completed Willis instrument for posterity. Certainly from the console, the sound of full organ would have been spectacular – the Great and Swell speaking straight to the player and the Pedal reeds in the loft within reach of the console! This instrument remained in service until 1919.

Our journey along the organ's time-line brings us to the unhappy time when World War One was fiercely raging.

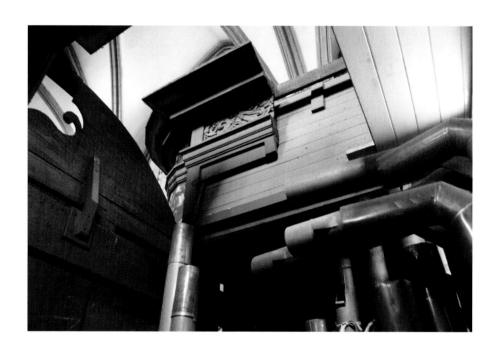

x : Internal picture of the South-East tower of the case, showing where the old case was divided and expanded by Willis. In the foreground are the Great reeds with Pedal pipes behind

CHAPTER THREE
HARRISON AND HARRISON:
THE ENGLISH ROMANTIC ORGAN: 1920 - 1969

Following the Great War, the condition of the Willis instrument gradually deteriorated, due in the main to almost continuous dusty work on the vaulting, with scaffolding up to the ceilings of the choir and transepts. Lengthy and dusty work had also prevailed during the years between 1912 and 1914 – enough to ruin any instrument.

Brewer had on numerous occasions raised the matter with the Dean and Chapter until at last, in 1917 he was given permission to discuss matters with Messrs Harrison and Harrison of Durham. Arthur Harrison was to oversee the work at Gloucester. He insisted on perfection in his voicing and it was his warm, rich and exquisitely blended tones that became the hallmark of the Harrison and Harrison brand.

As well as cleaning the instrument, Brewer wanted the pitch to be lowered to French pitch – this task alone costing £400. Brewer's vision however went further: he desired not simply a fully repaired organ but an instrument as beautiful and complete as modern craftsmanship could make it. A specification was drawn up by Harrison and Harrison and Brewer immediately approached his friends to enlist their support.

xi : Arthur Harrison

Within days, Sir James and Lady Horlick wrote to Brewer offering to undertake the entire expense of enlarging and reconstructing the organ at an estimated cost of £2,600. This generous donation was to be in memory of their son, Major Gerald Horlick, who had been killed in the war.

A number of new and expensive stops were added including the 32 foot Double Open Wood which found its home in the north triforium, complete with its own blowing plant. This was a wide-scale octave extending down to CCCC, underpinning the 16 foot Bishop pedal pipes, still positioned under the northern arch of the nave, but soon to be painted a shade of cream to blend with the Norman stone-work.

The Father Willis instrument was last played on 9th March 1920, after which dismantling began. Incredibly it may seem today, after only eight months, the new instrument was ready. On the afternoon of 19th November 1920, Sir James and Lady Horlick, standing beside the pillar on which is fixed a memorial brass, presented the instrument to the Dean and Chapter "to the glory of Almighty God". A programme of music was then presented by Brewer to a packed Cathedral. Later that evening, Brewer gave a full inauguration recital to a Cathedral again filled to overflowing in both nave and quire. What a great occasion this must have been – the like of which is so rarely witnessed today. Listening to the recital, indeed probably assisting, would have been the young Herbert Sumsion who the year before, had taken up the post of Assistant Organist under Brewer. Sumsion remained at Gloucester with Brewer until 1922, and then returned as Organist and Master of Choristers in 1928 following Brewer's sudden death. Little wonder then that this Harrison and Harrison instrument came to be regarded as Dr Sumsion's instrument, in whose personal care, from 1928 to 1967 when he retired, the only work carried out was to adjust the pitch again and brighten up the Tuba. A great testament to Harrisons' work and Sumsion's stewardship.

It was this Harrison organ with which I became intimately acquainted from the age of nine. I sang with it as a chorister, under Sumsion, daily for four years. Then, as a young teenager I was privileged to be able to practise on it almost any time I wished. I used to call round to the Organist's house (by this time John Sanders was Organist and Master of the Choristers) after boarding supper, pick up the keys to the Cathedral, enter by the north-west door and have the Cathedral and organ to myself. What a joy that was. I still remember the noise of the organ starting up in the dark silence of the building. There were hissings, cracks, bangs and what I felt resembled the sound of the awakening of a great beast from the depth of its slumbers. Gradually these noises died away as the reservoirs filled up and one was left with a gentle, familiar wind sound as the instrument told the player that it was ready for action. We were not supposed to start up the 32 foot blower way up in the quire triforium, but who would ever know? It strikes me that the sounds of a 747 jet airliner starting its engines must have been modelled on the sounds of the Gloucester Harrison on start-up! These days, alarms, insurance policies and health and safety regulations would doubtless prevent a 14-year-old undertaking such thrilling Harry Potter-like adventures, alone in an English cathedral.

Here is the specification, drawn up by Brewer, with Harrison and Harrison:

PEDAL ORGAN, 10 Stops, 4 *Couplers*

			FEET
1. Double Open Wood	(18 from No. 2)	Wood	32
2. Open Wood		Wood	16
3. Open Diapason	(from No. 17)	Metal	16
4. Sub Bass		Wood	16
5. Dulciana	(from No. 11)	Metal	16
6. Octave Wood	(18 from No. 2)	Wood	8
7. Flute	(18 from No. 4)	Wood	8
8. Ophicleide		Metal	16

| 9. Bassoon | (from No. 48) | Metal | 16 |
| 10. Posaune | (18 from No. 8) | Metal | 8 |

I. Choir to Pedal   *II. Great to Pedal*   *III. Swell to Pedal*
VI. Solo to Pedal

CHOIR ORGAN, 6 Stops, 2 *Couplers*

		FEET
11. Contra Dulciana	Metal	16
12. Viola da Gamba	Metal	8
13. Claribel Flute	Wood	8
14. Dulciana	Metal	8
15. Lieblich Flute	Metal	4
16. Harmonic Piccolo	Metal	2

V. Swell to Choir   *VI. Solo to Choir*

GREAT ORGAN, 13 Stops, 3 *Couplers*

		FEET
17. Double Open Diapason	Metal	16
18. Open Diapason, I	Metal	8
19. Open Diapason, II	Metal	8
20. Open Diapason, III	Metal	8
21. Claribel Flute	Wood	8
22. Octave	Metal	4
23. Harmonic Flute	Metal	4
24. Octave Quint	Metal	$2\frac{2}{3}$
25. Super Octave	Metal	2
26. Sesquialtera, 17. 19. 22	Metal	iii rks
27. Trombone	Metal	16
28. Trumpet	Metal	8
29. Clarion	Metal	4

VII. Choir to Great   *VIII. Swell to Great*   *IX. Solo to Great*

SWELL ORGAN, 13 Stops, *Tremulant and 2 Couplers*

		FEET
30. Lieblich Bourdon	Wood and Metal	16
31. Open Diapason	Metal	8
32. Lieblich Gedeckt	Metal and Wood	8
33. Salicional	Metal	8
34. Vox Angelica (ten. C)	Metal	8

35. Principal	Metal	4
36. Fifteenth	Metal	2
37. Mixture, 17. 19. 22	Metal	iii rks
38. Oboe	Metal	8
39. Vox Humana	Metal	8
	X. Tremulant	
40. Contra Posaune	Metal	16
41. Cornopean	Metal	8
42. Clarion	Metal	4

XI. Octave　　　　　　　*XII. Sub Octave*

SOLO ORGAN, 8 Stops, *Tremulant and 3 Couplers*

		FEET
43. Quintaton	Wood and Metal	16
44. Harmonic Flute	Metal	8
45. Concert Flute	Metal	4
46. Viole d'Orchestre	Metal	8
47. Viole Celeste	Metal	8
48. Orchestral Bassoon	Metal	16
49. Clarinet	Metal	8

XIII. Tremulant

Nos. 43 to 49 in the Solo box

| 50. Tuba (harmonic) | Metal | 8 |

XIV. Octave　　　　*XV. Sub Octave*　　　　*XVI. Unison off*

Nos. 43 and 48 had extra octaves for use with *XIV* and *XVI*, and were controlled by two pistons labelled "Quintaton, 8ft" and "Orchestral Hautboy, 8ft" respectively.

COMBINATION COUPLERS
XVII. Great and Pedal combinations coupled　　　*XVIII. Pedal to Swell combinations*

ACCESSORIES
Six combination pedals to the Pedal organ
Three combination pistons to the Choir organ
Six combination pistons to the Great organ
Six combination pistons to the Swell organ
Six combination pedals to the Swell organ (duplicating pistons)
Six combination pistons to the Solo organ

Reversible piston to No. 8
Reversible pedal to *Great to Pedal*
Reversible piston to *Great to Pedal*
Reversible piston to *Swell to Great*
Reversible foot piston to Swell *Tremulant*
Reversible foot piston to Solo *Tremulant*
Two balanced crescendo pedals to Swell and Solo organs
Wind Pressures:-
Pedal flue-work, 4 and 4½ inches; reeds, 6 and 15 inches
Choir, 3½ inches
Great flue-work, 4 and 6 inches; reeds, 7 inches
Swell flue-work, Oboe and Vox Humana, 4½ inches; other reeds, 7 inches
Solo flue-work and orchestral reeds, 6 inches; Tuba, 15 inches
Action wind, 10 inches

xii : The Harrison Console

The draw-stop jambs were at an angle of 45 degrees to the keyboards. The stop-handles had solid ivory heads, the speaking stops being lettered in black, and the couplers, etc. (indicated above by italics), in red. The latter were grouped with the speaking stops of the departments they complemented. The combination pistons had solid ivory heads.

Harrisons re-used parts of the Willis console – the white manual keys and the uniquely Willis round-fronted sharps. But they had to change the physical layout of the Willis instrument to accommodate their enlargements: the Solo box was removed from behind the console to the space alongside the staircase, with the Pedal Ophicleide and its Posaune extension standing in front of the shutters. The great case itself remained in its enlarged Willis state, its west front perched on the parapet of the screen.

The builder's latest Tubular Pneumatic system was applied to all the action except the manual to pedal couplers, which remained mechanical. In the new pipe-work, spotted metal was used for all trebles, harmonic, covered, and cone-tuned pipes. Blowing was by two electric fan motors (crypt and quire triforium).

This new Harrison was not simply an enlarged Willis. It had its own distinctive personality and I invite the reader to come back with me and share memories of some of its more famous sounds and idiosyncrasies.

I developed a keen interest in tape recording at the age of thirteen when my father purchased a recorder. So I used to walk around the Cathedral during Sumsion's Sunday Evensong voluntaries to try to discover the best recording position for the instrument should I ever have the chance to make a recording. (In those days, such an activity required the express permission of the Dean and of Dr Sumsion and was, sadly, hardly ever granted!) But the sound characteristics I discovered, confused me. The best sound was neither in the nave nor quire, but at the top of the steps leading into the south transept! What I was hearing was the result of Willis having turned his soundboards so that they ran east/west – during the second of his rebuilds which remained unchanged by Harrisons. The sound produced, projected predominantly to the south and north. There was also no roof to the Harrison instrument, so the sound, in the remarkable eight-second full organ echo, bounced up to the nave vault, down to the north and south – sounding "awesome" as we say today, at the console! This was hardly perfect for nave and quire services, but the high wind pressures and sheer decibel output made up for it. After all, this was a comparatively small cathedral organ, but the acoustic made it sound much larger.

This organ had many beautiful refinements, typical of Arthur Harrison's work. The reeds and flutes of the Solo division were perfect examples of their type whilst the Quintaton produced some unusual but beautiful bell-like harmonic effects. The Choir organ had a beautiful Claribel Flute which, with its bigger brother on the Great, were favourites of Sumsion. He would typically start all his improvisations either with these stops, the Swell strings or the Swell Open Diapason – box closed of course.

There were of course, limitations. The Pedal division, comprising ten stops from three extended ranks, none above 8 foot pitch, meant that clarity here was lacking. The Solo Tuba, positioned high in the south side of the case and speaking south produced a huge, if rather hooty sound. Sumsion invariably used it coupled to the pedals where he needed increased bite for loud pedal entries – such as the final pages of Bach fugues, played always in his "orchestral" style. It also provided good antiphonal effects with full Great, ably demonstrated in Sumsion's EMI recording of the Elgar Sonata. The Great number 1 Open Diapason was of a huge scale and Tibia-like in tone. Its addition to full organ tended to cause unpleasant thickness, adding volume (or din) rather than clarity. In contrast, the Great Diapason chorus built on the number 2 Open Diapason was well crafted and provided bright piercing colours. The frustration was that there was really no other chorus which the player could produce to balance it. The 32 foot Double Open Wood used to catch the acoustic and a sustained note from this octave seemed to amplify itself as it was held down. Sumsion regularly used the 32s for certain psalm verses, and on his EMI recording it gets a brief but effective outing during the Howells *Rhapsody*. We can also hear them on the enclosed CD, towards the close of Whitlock's *Folk Tune*.

It is easy to detail the shortcomings of any instrument, but of its type, this was a very fine organ much loved by the Gloucester congregations and especially by young enthusiastic cathedral choristers! The routine for probationers on Sunday afternoons was to sit in the organ loft for Evensong, as the choir-stalls would be full. Here we watched, often in amazement, as Dr Sumsion drove his 'Bentley' through the service with ease and totally relaxed confidence. During the lessons and sermons, he would practise his pedal scales whilst making notes on sheets of music – we would be treated to demonstrations of pedal octave unison scales or scales in contrary motion, always chromatic and seemingly unconsciously performed even while he was speaking quietly to us to run errands. During the voluntaries, we would all rush to the stairs in the hope that the Ophicleide would start up – a routine which has probably by now, resulted in some hearing loss among Gloucester Old Choristers of our vintage.

By the time Dr Sumsion retired in 1967 and John Sanders returned from Chester to take up the post of Organist and Master of the Choristers, subtle changes could be detected. The first I remember was that the "pedal 6" piston now brought out the 32 foot stop – a registrational adjustment which would never have happened during Sumsion's reign, but John Sanders was looking for a richer sound. Sadly though, the organ gradually became "asthmatic" – that friendly wind sound which comforted me during my practice evenings now began to sound like a terminal illness. The instrument became temperamental – the Pedal Ophicleide stop used to pop out of its own accord until eventually it simply would not go back in unless strong adhesive tape were applied. Things were not looking good and our 'Bentley' was heading for an MOT failure. It had given nearly fifty years of trouble-free service, but by the close of 1968 it was clear that something had to be done. Picture xiii shows the layout of the Harrison instrument. The Bishop pipes under the arch, the Solo box and the Pedal Ophicleide in front are all clearly visible. The console was attached to the south side of the case and the beautiful characteristic Harris arches were filled in with cloth-covered boarding to hide the pneumatic action.

xiii : The Harrison Organ in 1967 from the Triforium

CHAPTER FOUR
HILL, NORMAN & BEARD:
THE NEW GLOUCESTER ORGAN: 1970 – 2000

DESIGNING AND PLANNING

The organ we hear today is almost exactly the same instrument which emerged from the transformation begun in 1970, and which was completed in time for the Gloucester Three Choirs Festival in 1971. I say "almost exactly" as there have been more recent improvements described in the next chapter. But the character and personality remain the product of the 1970 vision.

It would be misleading simply to describe the 1970 work as merely rebuilding. What we witnessed was restoration, re-modelling and the creation of a completely new tonal design. Back in the early 70s, the English neo-classical organ building movement was at its height. The movement had begun in England in the 1950s with the Royal Festival Hall instrument, designed by Ralph Downes and built by Harrison and Harrison. This instrument caused uproar, controversy and delight - people simply loved or hated it. In subsequent years, Downes had gone on to successfully rebuild other major liturgical instruments such as those in the Brompton Oratory and St. Albans Cathedral. But his transformation of the Gloucester instrument was among the bravest and most controversial of the rebuilding of any English cathedral organ to this day.

In 1968, the Harrison and Harrison organ at Gloucester had played its part in the Three Choirs Festival, but its condition and behaviour determined John Sanders, the recently appointed Organist and Master of the Choristers, that a major project would be essential for the 1971 Festival. John was familiar with the Festival Hall organ and knew its designer and curator – Ralph Downes. He had on one occasion commented to Downes that something like the Festival Hall organ would sound wonderful in Gloucester Cathedral with its famous acoustic. It should not have been a surprise therefore when Ralph Downes was appointed by the Dean and Chapter in 1969 as consultant to the new organ project. The Dean at the time was the much respected Seiriol Evans who took some persuading that the proposed transformation was the right approach but who, once won over to the vision, supported Downes and Sanders tirelessly and tenaciously. Dean Evans wrote a foreword for the organ booklet published in 1971 which perfectly set the scene for this famous transformation:

"THE REBUILDING of a great Cathedral organ is an undertaking of considerable magnitude, and it was felt by the Dean and Chapter that, in the present understanding of organ design, it would not be enough merely to replace what was worn out and leave the character of the instrument as it had been since the rebuild by Willis nearly a century ago. It was therefore decided to engage Mr. Ralph Downes, C.B.E., whose reputation as an organ consultant is well known, to re-design our organ, and to bring it into line with musical thought about the function and capacity of organs at the present day. The builders chosen were Messrs. Hill, Norman and Beard. The Organs Advisory Committee of the Council for Care of Churches has approved both the specification of the organ and the repair of the case. It was found that the display pipes in the organ case had been painted in the reign of Charles II, though a coating of brown varnish concealed most of the detail. This was stripped off by the Honble. Miss Anna Plowden and Mr. Peter Smith, and the pipes now appear in their pristine beauty for all to see. All who commission or design work in a great Cathedral are making provision for future generations and thus carry a heavy load of responsibility, and this applies to an organ rebuild as much as to anything else. There are fashions in organ building, and all that can be done is to make sure that the most advanced thinking and the best craftsmanship are put into the job. And so our rebuilt organ is not a re-hash of bygone ideas, but an organ of the seventies, and as such it must be appraised.

SEIRIOL EVANS, *Dean 1970*

After considering a number of designs and quotations the firm of Hill, Norman and Beard was awarded the contract to build the new instrument to Downes' specification which reflected John Sanders' vision for a new, clear and focused sound projecting directly into the nave and quire and not to the north or south! Ralph Downes provided much needed support for John Sanders who not only had his exacting day job in a busy cathedral, but who was also planning and preparing for the 1971 Festival – no small task!

The new Gloucester organ was to fulfil the following demands:
1. accompany daily services in the quire
2. support the singing of large nave and quire congregations
3. accompany both chorus and orchestras of varying dimensions, and
4. perform solo recitals and concertos of various styles and periods

In a perfect world these demands would mean having two separate organs; a small one for daily services in the quire and a larger more powerful one in the nave. But at Gloucester, the Dean and Chapter were firm in their vision that there should be one organ only.

Downes initially took two considerations to the Dean and Chapter. The first was the retention of the *status quo* in all respects, with only a restoration of the mechanism and perhaps one or two alterations to the Choir organ. The second involved a completely new design in which the old cases and facade pipes should be given pride of place, the pipes being properly reinstated after their 80 years' silence. The whole instrument was to be housed within the cases, excepting only the large 16-foot Bishop Pedal pipes which would be once more withdrawn out of sight within the stone screen. The internal pipes of three complete original stops and fragments of six others from the 17th and 18th centuries were also to be reinstated to contribute to the new tonal scheme. Thus the instrument would have one distinctive voice and musical personality. The Dean and Chapter decided on the second consideration and the work commenced.

The design of the new instrument reduced the total bulk of the organ. The great case, which had been deepened over the years and which rested in an unsightly manner on the parapet of the screen, was reduced in depth to better architectural and aesthetic effect. The lowest twelve 32 foot Pedal Double Open Wood pipes which did not fit the new Downes scheme were disconnected. Instead of using 'loud' and 'soft' stops, Downes favoured the principle that every stop, *"though mild in tone, is so integrated with its fellows as to produce an ensemble possessing power, transparency, vitality and vivacity"*.

As the blueprint for the new organ emerged, the following characteristics became clear:
1. the organisation of the whole instrument would be on the *Werkprinzip*, namely, each division being a complete organ, encased in its own tone cabinet
2. the organisation of each division would be on the basis of a Principal chorus, a wide-scale flute chorus and reed stops
3. an open outlook would be created for all divisions, down the main axis of the building, and
4. 'full wind' voicing would be adopted for all pipes, on a pressure of air appropriate to the overall acoustics

PLANS BECOME REALITY

Hill, Norman and Beard (HN&B) carried out the work between 1969 and 1971, making the Downes scheme a reality. The Cathedral witnessed a new father and son team working on the project – Herbert Norman and his son, John. The work and responsibilities were divided such that Herbert Norman would concentrate on the case and structure whilst John Norman would be responsible for the new action and the manufacturing and voicing of the pipes.

They were faced with an interesting example of the English practice of perpetual rebuilding. Structurally this was a Father Willis, with a 17th century case tacked into position around it, with an early

20th century console. But as well as the two beautiful antique cases, there was a substantial collection of original Thomas Harris pipes which were renovated and incorporated into the new instrument. They were:

Front Open Diapason	8ft, from GG complete, the lowest 29 in the East case
Back Open Diapason	8ft, from GG complete save the top octave, the lowest 29 in the West case
Stopped Diapason	8ft, 17 wooden pipes from CC#
Front Principal	4ft, from GG (no GG#) nearly complete, the lowest 6 in the East case
Back Principal	4ft, 6 pipes in the West case
Stopped Flute	4ft, 9 wooden pipes from CC
Twelfth	2ft, 31 pipes from CC
Fifteenth	2ft, 12 pipes from CC
Mixture	33 pipes
Choir Principal	4ft, 14 speaking case pipes from GG to Tenor C (no low G#, A#, B or C#) plus one central dummy pipe (replacing a pipe speaking FF in the pre-Commonwealth organ) and 24 gilded wooden dummy pipes.

Many of the front pipes had been disconnected and used as dummies and the larger ones had had their backs cut out and spoke five notes higher than originally intended. Picture xv shows the back of some of the Harris West Diapason pipes, having been restored, their cut out sections having been made good.

xv : backs of Harris West Open Diapason – made good by HN&B

The inside pipes had been distributed across the instrument. The Twelfth, for instance, had become the treble of the Swell Open Diapason. In nearly every case the pipes had been transposed several notes higher, thus increasing the power, and a slot cut in the top to restore some harmonics. Fortunately, the mouths of these pipes had not been altered (cut up) so they were able to be restored. The biggest challenge these old pipes presented was that of identification. Many had been remarked four or five times, some transposed more than once and only by hours of examination could the faint original markings be recognised and deciphered. This was particularly true of the front pipes, many of which had been changed round at some time and replaced in the wrong positions. HN&B were able to check the original pitch from some of the unaltered but long-silent smaller front pipes, and found to their relief it was almost exactly the same as modern standard pitch. They were made of a lean spotted metal (approximately 35% tin) planed up to a flat surface on the outside. The restoration saw them carefully extended to their original lengths with similar metal.

The pipes of the East and West Diapasons and the Octave 4-foot of the Great are almost completely from the Thomas Harris organ: other smaller groups of Harris pipes have found their home in the Great Bourdon, Flute, Quartane and Mixture: the Choir Principal bass is also original.

In the new instrument the manual soundboards were returned back through 90 degrees, to sit once again parallel to the cases as in the original design, and the depth of the organ reduced to one department. The Great Organ is set in the centre of the main case and consists of three sections, one speaking east and one west, with the reeds between them.

xvi : west Great pipes

The Pedal Organ is placed either side of the Great Organ at the same level, except for the Bishop Pedal pipes and later additions. The Swell Organ is placed in the lower part of the case also speaking both east and west. It is fitted with separate expression pedals to control the sound in each direction. The Choir Organ speaks only into the quire so the West Positive Organ was provided on the nave side. This is played from the fourth manual and serves a broadly similar purpose in the Nave to that of the Choir Organ in the chancel, though with emphasis on orchestral continuo rather than choir accompaniment.

xvii : Great and Pedal reeds (Willis/HN&B)

Until the 1970 rebuild the case had no roof. To protect the pipes from direct sunlight which plays havoc with tuning, the cases were roofed. This allowed prompt reflection of sound from inside the tone-cabinets, giving a more precise and focused tone, rather than allowing it to waft up to the vault and back. Indeed, the resonance of the tone-cabinets so formed imparted a warmth and breadth to the tone of the relatively small-scaled Harris Diapasons that they would otherwise lack. This was the first English Cathedral organ to make use of the historic principle of separate tone cabinets for each department clearly visible in the case, itself only one department deep. However, more reference to the roof will be made in the following chapter.

To have accommodated an instrument of 55 stops almost entirely within a case only 10ft 6ins by 16ft is something of a record in compactness, especially when one considers that the old organ substantially overflowed a deepened case, though it had fewer stops.

xviii : east Great pipes

This economy of space was achieved largely by the compactness of a brand new electro-magnetic action, invented by John Norman and pioneered by HN&B for the Gloucester organ. This permitted the Swell and West Positive departments to occupy the space taken up by bellows and pneumatic action in the old organ. To the player, the action is considerably more rapid than conventional electro-pneumatic action and was in 1971 predicted to have a probable working life comparable with that of mechanical action. Other features of the construction of the organ included aluminium-faced swell shutters of solid laminated timber and the provision of combination pistons on the console adjustable on the Hill Norman & Beard capture system.

In addition to the Thomas Harris pipes, the few eighteenth century pipes in the organ were retained, together with the 1830 pedal pipes by Bishop. The Willis reeds were retained and revoiced with new shallots to fit their function in the new design. The remainder of the pipework was new, including pipes of spotted metal, tin metal, brass (Pedal Shawm), and copper. The pipe scales and general voicing treatment were determined, like the stop-list, by Ralph Downes, who had more experience of the scaling and voicing of neo-classical organs than any Englishman alive at the time. HN&B working in partnership with Downes was an automatic meeting of minds as Downes' approach to the organ and general voicing ideals coincided so closely with theirs. Downes took fastidious care over the voicing of the whole instrument to the extent that, for example, he set the wind pressure of the Choir Organ so that the Stopped Diapason exactly matched the voice of a cathedral chorister soloist.

The design and voicing of the new organ was conceived not only as an extension of the historic pipes, but as that of a modern instrument designed on the classical principles of organ design laid down in the 17th and 18th centuries. It incorporated features of the various national schools and provided for the performance of the more romantic music of the 19th and 20th centuries into an instrument which, although eclectic in its versatility, nevertheless still today speaks as with a single and unique personality. The full specification of the organ appears at the conclusion of chapter six.

REACTIONS

Paul Hale, writing in *Organists' Review* in May 2000, perfectly summed up people's response to this unique instrument: *"This organ has attracted praise and puzzlement in probably equal proportion during its thirty years of life"*. On first hearing the instrument, having been brought up on the Harrison, I have to admit to being shocked. Shocked by the directness of speech, by the brilliant mixtures, by the reeds which sounded so different in their new incarnation but delighted with the stunning sound of full organ which was more than adequate for the building's acoustic.

xix : John Sanders at the HN&B console, 1973

John Sanders introduced me to his new instrument in the mid–70s, following a Saturday Evensong which he accompanied at which were sung canticles Kelly in C and the anthem *God is gone up* by Finzi. The organ sounded terrifically exciting! Watching him play, particularly in the psalms, I was struck by how few stops he used to accompany the choir, using the more traditional stops as 'solos' throughout – the Great Diapasons, the Bourdon, Spitzflute and a combination of Flutes and Mutations from the West Positive to sound like a solo Clarinet from days gone by. My impression of the instrument was one of being utterly delightful to sing with – the results of Downes' painstaking voicing. Sanders explained that if one were looking for a standard issue cathedral organ here (he later used the phrase "vanilla flavoured" to describe the sameness of so many cathedral organ sounds of those days) one would be a little disappointed. Indeed he went further explaining that if the player tried to register as a 'standard' cathedral organ, the sound produced would be dull – e.g. Swell to mixture / reeds etc. I asked about the absence of a traditional Solo division and his comment was that there were solo stops everywhere – far more choice than had previously been the case; the player simply had to experiment with a new approach to registration. However, he did regret the absence of a big solo reed: there was simply no room for one in the case and at the time, insufficient funding.

I made many visits to hear the organ in the '80s and '90s and to speak to the incumbent Assistant Organists who discovered highly imaginative sounds never before heard – the late John Clough, Andrew Millington, Mark Blatchly and Mark Lee. I am fortunate to have in my collection many BBC broadcasts of Choral Evensongs, during which one can hear what a superb instrument this is for accompanying the choir. However, it was Mark Blatchly who made the instrument so popular with the general public, attracting many hundreds of people to his lunch–time recitals to raise money for choir tours. Amusingly, it is his improvisation on *Nellie the Elephant* rather than his wonderful interpretations of Messiaen which people seem to remember best. Sometimes there's no (musical) justice! Writing in *Organists' Review* in 2005 Mark commented:

"Let it be said that Gloucester Cathedral got a bold and thrilling Downes organ in 1971 because John Sanders knew what he wanted, and would settle for nothing less. Its beauty, its strength of character and the Romantic nature of its warm foundations and reeds struck me from the first..."

Kindly summing up his thoughts for this book, Mark proclaims the Gloucester organ as being "the best organ and building combination in the known world, first equal with Notre-Dame de Paris, Arundel Cathedral and Liverpool Metropolitan", concluding his thoughts to me with "... dull and personality-deficient organs seemed to me to be the norm in this country with the exception of a few 'belters' such as Hexham, Coventry, St. Albans, the Festival Hall and a few others, standing out from the mumbling crowd. How lucky we are at Gloucester! Hurrah for Downes and Sanders!"

I am delighted to include similar praise from Ashley Grote, the present Assistant Director of Music.

"There can be no other Cathedral organ whose voice is so distinctive. A recent visitor to the loft remarked that, listening to a broadcast of choral evensong, he could recognise it instantly to be Gloucester thanks to the sound of the organ and of course the generous acoustic. The organ and the building are as one, a perfect relationship of architecture and sound. I sometimes take the opportunity to remind myself of this by sitting by the Great West Door during an evening organ recital. As one looks up, one cannot help but be moved by the sight of that magnificent painted case, framed in silhouette by the vast East window, standing majestically at the heart of the building. The sound of the organ envelops every corner of the Cathedral, speaking powerfully and clearly yet with a warmth and richness.

It is true to say that in order to accompany a choir successfully in the standard Anglican choral repertoire on the Gloucester organ, one has to adopt an imaginative and creative approach to registration.

Handled with care, it can impersonate many of the sounds associated with Anglican choral music, as well as being one of the most versatile and exciting instruments of any cathedral in the land. There are many cathedral organs that can accompany Stanford and Howells convincingly; almost none that can in addition produce such authentic sounding and powerful performances of Bach, Reger, Messiaen, Vierne or Duruflé.

What a privilege and a thrill it is to sit at the Gloucester organ each day. The challenges it presents only serve to make the job of playing it all the more interesting and exciting."

Not everyone had been quite so positive however. I remember talking to many old friends who still in the mid-80s missed the old Tuba (now enjoying life in the church of All Saints, Margaret Street, London) and the big rolling sound of the Harrison, but yet understood that the new instrument was a real step forward. The person who could conceivably have been most upset by the new tonal scheme was Dr Sumsion. In 1983 I asked him for his impression of the new organ. His response was that of the gentleman he truly always was: "I have no problem at all with what's there, but I was a little saddened by what was taken away."

Many more however have since fallen under the spell of the distinctive Gloucester sound, none more than David Briggs who succeeded John Sanders as Director of Music in 1994.

CHAPTER FIVE
NICHOLSON AND COMPANY: 2000 – 2010

David Briggs' early impressions of the Downes/Sanders instrument predate 1994 by many years. I am delighted to quote some of his memories, kindly shared with me for this book. David recalls:

"My very first impressions of the Gloucester organ were formed when, as a 14-year old, I travelled down by train from Birmingham (without telling my parents!) with my good friend John Butt, now Professor of Music at Glasgow University. I vividly remember stepping into that enormous nave for the first time – there was a memorial service in progress. This was the first time I'd ever experienced the marvellous Gloucester acoustic and was blown away by the sound of the instrument. We attended Evensong and afterwards Andrew Millington very kindly allowed both of us to have a few minutes on the instrument. John played a bravura performance of the Duruflé *Toccata* and I remember improvising away rather loudly and Andrew asking if I could come to a C major cadence before too long. I was struck by the vivacity and excitement of the sound. Some years later, when I was Assistant Organist at Hereford, I used to love hearing Mark Blatchly's uniquely inventive improvisations before the Three Choirs Festival Evensongs and in 1989 Mark very kindly invited me to give a concert. That was the first time I really got to know the instrument well. When I arrived as Director of Music in 1994, I could hardly keep off the instrument. It soon became an important constituent in my musical psyche, just as the Truro 'Father Willis' had six years earlier and it was a privilege to play the Gloucester organ for eight years, on an almost daily basis".

The Hill, Norman and Beard instrument gave superb service for 30 years, during which time the instrument had been regularly maintained. However, it became clear by 1998, that the action had started to fail to some degree. It was discovered that a number of the individual magnetic solenoids were simply wearing out. The failing magnets could have been replaced but the view was to renew them all for future generations. So, the decision was taken to renovate the entire instrument, replacing all the individual solenoids along with modernising the console. As Hill, Norman and Beard had ceased trading some years earlier, another company had to be employed. Nicholsons of Worcester were chosen to carry out the restoration, sourcing the new electro-magnets from Germany.

The opportunity was also taken at this time, to add a limited number of new Pedal ranks, thus 'completing' and strengthening the Pedal division. This work was overseen by David Briggs who wished that the Harrison 32-foot pipes had been preserved, but they had been destroyed prior to his being in post. He therefore considered how to restore the 32-foot components. There would be no room in the screen for a full length 32-foot, so Nicholsons provided a Cornet Separée of 32-foot harmonics – a Quint $10^2/3$ (from the existing Sub Bass); Tierce $6^2/5$ and Septieme $4^4/7$, which together create an illusion of 32-foot pitch.

xx : Looking into the stair well

Nicholsons made a fine job of modelling these on similar examples at Notre-dame de Paris and they lend great depth to the sound of the Pedal Organ. In addition, a 32-ft Bombarde (with half-length resonators) was placed within the screen. This stop adds real excitement to the full organ. Picture xx is taken looking down into the space on the north side of the case: bottom left – 32 foot Nicholson Bombarde; top centre – Bishop Flute 16 foot; metal pipes to the right are the Nicholson Pedal mutations.

Briggs also made a subtle change to the West Positive: the Larigot pipes were re-arranged to create a Septième. A Swell Sub Octave was added and the console was upgraded to include a stepper and a Pedal Divide, which increases the possibilities for multi-layering in repertoire and improvisation. The player can now have the sound from one (or more) of the manuals as a solo register in the top region of the Pedalboard, and retain the Pedal Foundation stops and couplers if required in the bass. In addition, the soundboards were renovated; a new solid state transmission was installed; provision made for an IBM-compatible replay system and new drawstop solenoids were provided.

The final change made at this time was that the central portion of the Great roof was removed and placed over the eastern third section. This allowed the nave vault once again to act as a sounding board as it had done in the Wills and Harrison days. There is no doubt that this has had a considerable effect on the sound of the instrument: it actually sounds larger now and the Great and Pedal reeds sound altogether richer. But some of the original focus of the sound has been sacrificed. However, as the sections of the roof are still in situ, they could easily be replaced if tastes and requirements change in future years.

A solo reed was seriously considered at this time, but there was real uncertainty as to where to place it. One option was to place it on a rotating turntable above the Bishop pipes, rather akin, as Briggs comments, to Thomas the Tank Engine's shunting yard mechanism! But in the end, the idea was shelved for another day.

xxi : The Console in 2010

Happily, as this book goes to print, a Trompette Harmonique solo reed will have just been installed by Nicholson and Co., thus finally 'completing' the organ. The new rank, with its booster blowing plant is to be placed at the north end of the space adjacent to the staircase, the pipes pointing up to the vault to reflect the sound both east and west. This rank will comprise 58 pipes of spotted metal (53% tin) on eight inch wind pressure. The design incorporates French domed shallots, in keeping with the style and tonal characteristics of the existing Great reeds. The three pictures overleaf were taken at the Nicholson factory as the new stop was being prepared. Guy Russell, Nicholson's Tonal Director kindly agreed to be featured.

*xxii : the booster blower
and wind regulator*

*xxiii : Guy Russell with
a new resonator*

*xxiv : three Cs being tested at
8-inch pressure*

This new stop will be available both on the West Positive and the Choir. In addition a Great Reeds on Choir transfer has been added.

One can only wonder what Ralph Downes might have thought of the new work in 2001 and 2010. Certainly John Sanders greatly approved of the Pedal developments, though he would not himself have had much use for the Swell Sub Octave. John had regretted the eventual removal of the Harrison 32 foot pipes, though he and Downes had considered incorporating a solo reed. So one assumes that the latest addition would have found much favour. Downes certainly favoured pedal mutations.

What we do know is that the Nicholson rebuild beautifully retained and enhanced the integrity of the Downes/Sanders instrument with craftsmanship and skill. We can only hope that if Ralph and John are looking down on today's organ at Gloucester, they will grant us the occasional smile for the way in which we cherish and continue to improve their stunning, unique and beautiful instrument.

CHAPTER SIX
THE ORGAN CASES

THE 1970 RESTORATION

The transformation of the organ during 1970 – 1971 saw the complete restoration of the two cases at Gloucester. Thankfully, these two old and beautiful cases, with their painted pipes were retained in situ during various rebuilds. Until 1970, most of the ancient painted display pipes had not spoken for over one hundred years and the case itself bore little connection with the Harrison instrument within it. The pipes and the cases had steadily deteriorated over the centuries. The cases are recognised as of great historical importance and beauty but until 1970, they scarcely received the attention that such rare survivals warranted.

xxv : the west front of the Organ

It had clearly been problematic for Harrisons to fit their organ into this once beautiful antique case designed for an instrument without pedals and with manuals of the old deep compass. Thus, for the 1970 transformation, it was considered as desirable to restore the original shape of the case as it was to restore the woodwork and painted decoration, effecting a comprehensive restoration. No original woodwork could be removed, or altered; and to regain something of the old proportions the main case had to be made shallower from east to west. This was achieved by raising it bodily, so that the Swell could be placed in the waist below the impost, but within the limits which would be observed if the Choir organ were still controlled by tracker action. As the west front had long presented a rather dumpy appearance, not helped by the side projections and its position at the edge of the screen, the effect achieved in 1971 was a huge improvement.

The structural restoration of the two ancient organ cases and the reversal of the historical process of continual enlargement posed many interesting challenges. Dismantling of the main case had to be avoided because of the fragile condition of the joinery. It would have been too precarious and would have risked extensive damage since almost everything was glued and located with a minimum of hand-made nails. The joints were further weakened by stresses arising from mild desiccation of the oak. As the entire interior frame had to be removed, the exterior was surrounded and secured by scaffolding. As the organ inside was removed, the case was braced also from the inside against collapse, particularly of the rudimentary structure of the lower parts.

Comparison of the structure of the two cases confirms that they are by two hands at different dates. The Chair case is sound and rigid, a fine construction in oak excellently joined by an expert cabinet maker over four hundred years ago. The Great case by contrast is bucolic joinery, relatively poorly constructed. It carries the considerable weight of the moulded upperwork, particularly the centre towers which, by 1969, had sunk and were falling. The west side is rather better made than the east although all the detail matches. At a former rebuilding two of the pilaster framed flats were unconcernedly pushed outwards many inches to create extra organ space inside, leaving ragged moulded mitres. Apart from the one preserved end panel (on the north side of the Great case) the side casing was a collection of miscellaneous soft wood joinery with nothing at all below parapet level.

Bringing the Great case back into logical use imposed a strict but beneficial discipline, as it is no longer an inflated screen to the visible organ parts. This case has become an outward expression of the internal layout and a functional part of it. The east to west depth was reduced to 125 inches, and the west face now stands free of the parapet. With the pillared open corners unblocked, a new elegance of profile replaces the former dumpy aspect from the nave.

xxvi : Organ from the nave before 1968

Below impost level, much of the original case was totally missing. Where original work remained, however truncated or vestigial, it was re-used in the reconstruction, with new work to make up the balance. Research into the original vertical relationship of the Great and Chair cases proved inconclusive possibly because of 19th century changes when the floor was strengthened. Even so it was difficult to see how choir trackers under the floor and later, a pedal board, could have been provided in the low space under the remnants of the key rail. Ultimately it was visual considerations alone which decided the precise 16 inches that the main case was bodily raised to make a sensible and practical part of the new interior layout.

The removal from sight of the huge scale wooden pipes blocking the north arch to the pulpitum opened up a new vista of the case and the old end panel.

Although of oak, the east and west facades are painted and grained. Formerly a medium brown tint, this finish had darkened with time but still looked handsome after cleaning and wax brushing. There were some traces of past gold enrichments and evidence that the choir case was formerly white painted with gold pointing and shading.

Restoration involved checking every joint, making secure and reducing strains from sagging joinery; always having in mind the stresses that future standards of church heating would have on this ancient but still lively material. Missing parts and damaged ornaments were made good.

CASE DETAILS

The work of restoring all the painted decoration was carried out by the Honble. Miss Anna Plowden and Mr. Peter Smith, with the aid of a generous grant from the Pilgrim Trust. The cases and pipes continue today to delight us with the uninhibited colours of Restoration England. Herbert Norman, of HN&B, added to the dignity of the cases by designing and installing the grilles under the four corner arches and that in front of the West Positive pipes.

The unique opportunity to examine standing antique organ cases in detail inside and out was revealing. Certainly the Great case was originally only 50 inches deep, the cornice mouldings were just cut midway and increasingly longer insertions made at each rebuilding until it was no less than 150 inches deep. The only remaining 17th century end panel now at the north-east corner confirms this.

The Chair case has a delicacy of detail and grace of outline which is not found in the Great case which is by contrast heavier in outline and whose detail revels in the joys of the countryside – leaves, trees, and flowers on backgrounds of various base colours. On the sides of the Chair case are pendants which are early 17th-century in feeling. The curved plan of the flats, the restrained mouldings, the treatment of the centre tower all point to such a date. The pipes in the flats are late 17th-century gilded wooden dummies and the tall centre pipe of the middle tower has never spoken. This could support the theory that this elegant case housed a one-manual organ of different compass to that placed in it by Harris in 1663-6, and that the original pipes of the front would be from a 4ft principal down to F. The construction is that of fine cabinet-work, while the Great case above is more the work of a provincial joiner.

Turning to the Great case, the west face was originally the 'back front' of the Harris instrument facing into the south transept, when the organ stood in the quire, and therefore relies on painted rather than carved decoration. Pipe-shades and cornices are covered with floral arabesques, in ochre-yellow with the highlights left in bare wood producing a bold effect.

The two largest pipes, those in the centre of each of the outer towers, have crowned monograms "C" and "R" respectively, for "Carolus Rex". These devices are repeated in the cornices of the tower caps. Much Victorian over-painting was removed from these two pipes

xxvii : Chair case pipes

xxviii : west case detail

to reveal cherubs' heads, mantling and grotesque seated figures in Phrygian caps. The painting on the pipes generally is on grounds of white, dark green and vermilion, with scrolls and flower-heads, sometimes arranged as strapwork or tassels, and with the edges shaded in black to give a three-dimensional effect. There are reserve panels which include tulips, birds, oak-trees, roses, talbots, King David playing the harp, a lyre, and a young woman holding an apple.

On the east face of the Great case we see a brave display of heraldry— the coats-of-arms of James, Duke of York and Edward Hyde, Earl of Clarendon on the central pipes of the outer towers, and on the centre pipe of the central tower the arms granted in 1542 to "Trinitye Church of Gloucester". On a carved cartouche below the centre tower are painted the early arms of the Abbey of Gloucester.

xxix : west centre pipes

With the arms of Charles II this decoration amounted to a great Royalist manifesto, coinciding in date with the time of Charles II's greatest popularity.

The variety in the shapes of the pipe-mouths is typical of Harris' work, with fine raised French mouths for the largest pipes, ogee-headed mouths for some pipes in the smaller towers and pointed mouths for the remainder. The central tower of the east front main case is of an unusual plan and appears to be thrust slightly upward. The same feature—in the same position—occurs on Loosemore's case at Exeter, where there is documentary evidence that he went to Salisbury, the better to learn how to make the organ at Exeter. It is not unlikely that this feature was copied, both at Gloucester and Exeter, from the earlier organ at Salisbury; and the device of making the central tower of an eccentric shape is common to many organ cases before 1680. The open arches under the side towers are a feature which was found in the case at Worcester, and was copied later (in the 18th century) in West Country organs—that by Harris and Byfield formerly in St. Mary Redcliffe, Bristol, was a notable example.

The sides of the Great case were drastically altered when the organ was deepened by Willis, but during the 1970 restoration panelling formerly thrust asunder has been joined up and there is a carved frieze partly surviving at the level of the impost. The projecting cornices added in the 19th century have been brought back into line, and the three pipes now standing on each side were decorated in a style harmonising with that of the old fronts. These pipes feature the initials of those key people involved with the restoration and transformation of this wonderful instrument:

JDS – John Sanders, Organist and Master of the Choristers

CBC – Cecil Clutton (Sam) was originally called in by the Dean at the start of the project to offer initial advice. It is interesting to note that, whilst he correctly established the provenance of the cases, it was John Norman who discovered that so many Harris pipes had

xxx : North Case display pipes   *xxxi : South Case display pipes*

survived inside, having identified each of them, distributed throughout the Harrison instrument.

MJG – Michael Gillingham, a friend of Sam Clutton, eventually did all the research into the history of the instrument for the restoration project. Whilst he did not have an official position on the project team, he liaised closely with Herbert Norman on the casework.

HJN – this is actually John Norman, his first name being Herbert, as was his father's.

ABP – The Honble. Miss Anna Plowden who, with Peter Smith restored the paintwork of the Harris pipes and painted the display pipes in the north and south case flats.

PJS – Peter Smith

BJA – Bernard Ashwell, the Cathedral Architect

RWD – Ralph Downes

56

THE ORGAN OF GLOUCESTER CATHEDRAL
SPECIFICATION 2010

Compass: 4 Manuals CC–A, 58 notes Pedals CC–G 32 notes

All stops were new in 1971, unless otherwise indicated:

GREAT ORGAN

Gedecktpommer		16	
Open Diapason (East)		8	Harris
Open Diapason (West)		8	Harris
Spitzflute (West)		8	
Bourdon		8	Harris bass
Octave (East)		4	Harris
Prestant (West)		4	Harris bass
Stopped Flute		4	Harris bass
Flageolet		2	
Quartane (West)	II rks	$2^2/3$	partly Harris
Mixture	IV–VI rks	$1^1/3$	partly Harris
Cornet (mounted)	IV rks	4	(from middle C)
Posaune		16	Willis
Trumpet		8	Willis
Clarion		4	Willis

Mixture Compositions:

Quartane II	throughout	12. 15
Mixture IV–VI	CC – B	19. 22. 26. 29
	Tenor C – Tenor B	15. 19. 22. 22. 26
	Middle C – Middle F	12. 15. 15. 19. 22
	Middle F# – Middle B	8. 12. 15. 15. 19. 22
	Treble C – Treble B	8. 12. 12. 15. 15. 19
	Top C – Top A	8. 8. 12. 12. 15. 15
Cornet IV	Middle C up	8. 12. 15. 17

SWELL ORGAN

Chimney Flute		8	
Salicional		8	
Celeste		8	(from A)
Principal		4	
Open Flute		4	
Nazard		$2^2/_3$	
Gemshorn		2	
Tierce		$1^3/_5$	
Mixture	IV rks	1	
Cimbel	III rks	$^1/_5$	
Fagotto		16	Willis
Trumpet		8	Willis
Hautboy		8	partly Willis
Vox Humana		8	Willis
Tremulant			

Mixture Compositions:

Mixture IV	CC – A#	22. 26. 29. 33
	B – Ten G#	19. 22. 26. 29
	Tenor A – Middle F	15. 19. 22. 26
	Middle F# – Treble E	12. 15. 19. 22
	Treble F – Top D	8. 12. 15. 19
	Top D# – Top A	5. 8. 12. 15
Cimbel III	CC – EE	38. 40. 43
	FF – A	36. 38. 40
	A# – Tenor D	33. 36. 38
	Tenor D# – Tenor G	31. 33. 36
	Tenor G# – Middle C	29. 31. 33
	Middle C# – Middle F	26. 29. 31
	Middle F# – Middle A#	24. 26. 29
	Middle B – Treble D#	22. 24. 26
	Treble E – Treble G#	19. 22. 24
	Treble A – Top C	17. 19. 22
	Top C# – Top F	15. 17. 19
	Top F# – Top A	12. 15. 17

CHOIR ORGAN

Stopped Diapason		8	
Principal		4	Harris front pipes, new treble
Chimney Flute		4	
Fifteenth		2	
Nazard		$1^1/_3$	
Sesquialtera	II rks	$1^1/_3$	
Mixture	III rks	$^1/_2$	
Cremona		8	
Tremulant			
Trompette Harmonique		8	Nicholson 2010 (shared with Man.IV)

Mixture Compositions:

Sesquialtera II	CC – B	19. 24
	Tenor C – Top A	12. 17
Mixture III	CC – A	29. 33. 36
	A# – Tenor F	26. 29. 33
	Tenor F# – Middle D	22. 26. 29
	Middle D# – Middle A#	19. 22. 26
	Middle B – Treble G#	15. 19. 22
	Treble A – Top D	12. 15. 19
	Top D# – Top A	8. 12. 15

WEST POSITIVE ORGAN (Manual IV)

Gedecktpommer		8	
Spitzflute		4	
Nazard		$2^2/_3$	
Doublette		2	
Tierce		$1^3/_5$	
Septième		$1^1/_7$	(Nicholson 2000; 1971 Larigot $1^1/_3$)
Cimbel	III rks	$^1/_2$	
Tremulant			
Trompette Harmonique		8	Nicholson 2010 (shared with Choir)

Mixture Composition:

Cimbel III	CC – FF#	29. 36. 40
	G – Tenor D#	29. 33. 36
	Tenor E – Tenor A#	22. 29. 33
	Tenor B – Middle G	22. 26. 29
	Middle G# – Treble D	15. 22. 26
	Treble D# – Treble B	15. 19. 22
	Top C – Top E	8. 15. 19
	Top F – Top A	8. 12. 15

PEDAL ORGAN

Flute		16	Bishop
Principal		16	Willis and Harris bass; treble from West Diapason
Sub Bass		16	old pipes, maker uncertain
Quint (ext. Flute 16)		$10^2/_3$	Nicholson 1999
Octave		8	partly Harris case pipes
Stopped Flute		8	
Tierce		$6^2/_5$	Nicholson 1999
Septième		$4^4/_7$	Nicholson 1999
Choral Bass		4	Harrison
Open Flute		2	
Mixture	IV rks	$1^1/_3$	
Bombarde (ext. Bombarde 16)		32	Nicholson 1999
Bombarde		16	Willis
Trumpet		8	Willis
Shawm		4	

Mixture Composition:

Mixture IV	throughout	19. 22. 26. 29

COUPLERS

Swell Sub Octave	West Great Flues Sub Octave	
Swell to Great	West Positive to Great	Choir to Great
Swell to Choir	West Positive to Choir	
Great to Pedal	West Positive to Pedal	Choir to Pedal
Swell to Pedal		

TRANSFERS

Great Reeds on Manual IV   Great Reeds on Choir

West Great Flues on Manual IV

COMBINATION COUPLERS

Great and Pedal Combinations coupled   Generals on Swell Toe Pistons

PEDAL DIVIDE

Below dividing point: All Pedal Stops and Couplers

Above dividing point: Four illuminated controls (Choir /

                               Great / Swell / West Positive)

PISTONS

Eight thumb pistons to Great

Eight thumb pistons to Swell

Six thumb pistons to Choir

Four thumb pistons to West Positive

Two Stepper Advance thumb pistons and two Retard

Eight general thumb pistons

16 levels of divisional pistons and 384 levels of general pistons

Eight toe pistons to Pedal

Eight toe pistons duplicating Swell thumb pistons

One Stepper Advance toe piston and one Retard

Reversible thumb pistons to Swell to Great, West Positive to Great,

Great to Pedal, Swell to Pedal, Choir to Pedal, Man IV to Pedal

Reversible toe pistons to Swell to Great, Great to Pedal

General Cancel

Setter

OTHER PLAYING AIDS

Balanced mechanical pedals to: East Swell Shutters

                                 West Swell Shutters

CONSOLE

The console is of oak, as is the organ bench, the height being adjustable
by means of the HN&B rise and fall mechanism. Pedal keys of birch and
contrasting rosewood.

ORGANISTS OF GLOUCESTER CATHEDRAL

The known organists of the cathedral are listed below. Following John Sanders' retirement in 1994, the title of *'Organist and Master of the Choristers'* was changed to *'Director of Music'*.

1582   Robert Lichfield
1620   Elias Smith
1620   Philip Hosier
1638   Berkeley Wrench
1640   John Okeover
1662   Robert Webb
1665   Thomas Lowe
1666   Daniel Henstridge
1673   Charles Wren
1679   Daniel Rosingrave
1682   Stephen Jeffries
1710   William Hine
1730   Barnabas Gunn
1743   Martin Smith
1782   William Mutlow
1832   John Amott
1865   Samuel Sebastian Wesley
1876   Charles Harford Lloyd
1882   Charles Williams
1897   Sir Arthur Herbert Brewer
1928   Herbert Sumsion
1967   John Sanders
1994   David Briggs
2002   Andrew Nethsingha
2007   Adrian Partington

ACKNOWLEDGEMENTS

I would like to offer my sincere and grateful thanks to the many people who have helped me produce this booklet and the CD – a project which has taken a number of years. In particular, I must make special mention of the following:

Mark Blatchly for his sincere encouragement and his words which I have been delighted to include

David Briggs for donating two recordings for the CD and writing his appreciation of the instrument for the booklet

Simon Gibson and the team at EMI Classics at Abbey Road Studios for providing the two Sumsion Whitlock pieces for the CD

Ashley Grote for taking time out from his busy schedule to help me photograph the internal views of the instrument and for his comments which are included

Paul Hale for his careful proof-reading and kind advice on the accuracy of content

Chris Jeans, Archivist at Gloucester Cathedral for providing access to all cathedral documents relating to the organ

Andrew Nethsingha for donating a previously recorded movement for the CD and Gary Cole of Regent Records for his recording and editing

John Norman for his support and an initial recorded interview on the 1971 rebuild

Andrew Parker who kindly gave permission to use tracks of John Sanders' playing for the CD

Adrian Partington for his encouragement and his playing for the CD

Esther Platten for her superb colour photographs on the booklet covers

Guy Russell, Tonal Director of Nicholsons, for pictures and information on the new solo Trompette Harmonique

Grant Vicat for the loan of the Herbert Sumsion 78rpm record featured on the CD

Janet Sanders for her support, encouragement and providing photographs of John for the booklet

REFERENCES

Baroque Tricks
Ralph Downes, 1999. Positif press, Oxford

The Organ Magazine
Essay by Rev. Andrew Freeman on the organ of Gloucester Cathedral. July 1924

The Organ Quarterly
Essay by Herbert Byard on the Organ of Gloucester Cathedal. April 1972

Gloucester Cathedral Organ
A booklet published following the 1971 rebuilding of the Organ
Essays by Michael Gillingham; Herbert and John Norman; Ralph Downes

The Box of Whistles
John Norman, 2007. Azure Publications

Gloucester Cathedral Organ – 1999 refurbishment
Article by Paul Hale in the Organists' Review, May 2000. Sections reproduced with kind permission of the Incorporated Association of Organists

Gloucester Cathedral – its Organs and Organists
The Very Rev. Henry Gee. Chiswick Press 1921

CD PROGRAMME

HERBERT SUMSION

1. *Larghetto – S. S. Wesley*
2. *Chorale Prelude 'Come Sweet Death' – J. S. Bach*
Taken from a 78rpm shellac record, privately produced to raise money for the Widows and Orphans of the Clergy in 1949; kindly loaned by Grant Vicat. This mono recording has been remastered but surface noise from this elderly record can inevitably be heard.

xxxii : Herbert Sumsion 1967

3. *Folk Tune – Percy Whitlock*
4. *Scherzo – Percy Whitlock*
Recorded by EMI in 1965 and are reproduced here by kind permission of EMI Classics at Abbey Road Studios.

5. *Fugue in B minor, BWV544 – J. S. Bach*
From a BBC broadcast in 1967. This mono recording is from a reel-to-reel domestic recorder. There is some traffic interference and some tape hiss, but well worth including for Sumsion's style of Bach playing.
All tracks played by Sumsion are on the Harrison instrument.

JOHN SANDERS

6. *Allegretto – Charles H. Lloyd*
7. *Marche Funèbre et Chant Seraphique – Guilmant*
Recorded in 1980 by Andrew Parker and reproduced here by kind permission. The organ on these two tracks is the original Downes/ Sanders instrument from 1971.

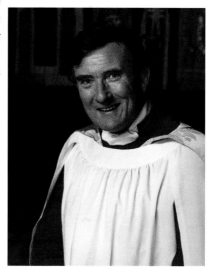

xxxiii : John Sanders

DAVID BRIGGS

8. Improvised Variations on Baa Baa Black Sheep
From a live concert in 1997 – the original Downes / Sanders instrument.
9. Final from Symphony No. 3 – Camille Saint-Saëns, transcribed By David Briggs
Recorded in 2001 on the Downes/ Sanders instrument as rebuilt by Nicholsons, minus the roof.
Tracks 9 and 10 are reproduced here by kind permission of David Briggs.

xxxiv : David Briggs

ANDREW NETHSINGHA

10. Organ Symphony No. 2; First Movement – Louis Vierne
Recorded by Gary Cole in 2006 and reproduced by kind permission.

ADRIAN PARTINGTON

11. *A Fancy – Thomas Tomkins*
12. *Prelude and Fugue in E flat – Camille Saint-Saëns*
13. *Trumpet Tune – Andrew Carter*

xxxv :
Andrew Nethsingha

Recorded in July 2010 by John Balsdon and Mark Hartt-Palmer. The organ is the Downes / Sanders / Nicholson instrument with the Trompette Harmonique installed and demonstrated in the final track.

xxxvi : Adrian Partington